Welcome

Take my hand and walk with me through the underbelly of my county jail. Meet the former corrections officer who severed his wife's head, a woman who claims she had oral sex with Trump and got nothing in return, the hopelessness of the mentally ill and the homeless, the suburban high school teacher pandering sexual material, inmates trying to escape through the ceiling tiles. It's all here, take a look.

Contents

April / May

Orientation

I had two weeks of training for my nursing job at the jail. I followed different nurses and watched what they did. It was rather amusing at that point; we seemed to have a lot of laughs. When I was out on my own it was a different story. I will never forget what my boss said in my interview. "When you leave for the day, your back won't hurt, and your feet won't hurt. It's all a mental thing." Those words have stayed with me, words of truth.

During the weeks of training many antics occurred. I was eating lunch at my desk when the officer radios went wild. An inmate in the intake department had scaled the wall and was on the loose in the ceiling. I didn't want him crashing down on my sandwich. Later I heard that he came against a wall and could go no further. He circled back, dropped down and was looking through the door at the officers staring at the ceiling. That made me feel safe.

I learned new medical techniques. The radio call came that an inmate was having a seizure. When we arrived at the cell, he was lying half on and half off the bed. We were told that earlier he placed a paper bag over his head to hyperventilate. The medic took his arms one at a time, lifted them and then let them drop. The arms fell away from his face. I learned that if he was truly unresponsive the arm would not protect his face. "I'm going to poke you in the eye. Are you ready?" There was enough of a response that the poke was not necessary. "He's faking all of this, he's fine." Our medical team left the scene.

While giving out medications with my preceptor, she told me about one of the inmates we were about to meet. He was formally a corrections officer at the jail. One day he snapped. He severed his wife's head. It was found in another room of the house. He attempted to sever his own head, but I could see by the scar that it was a lame attempt. When he was initially brought to jail, he kept saying "She will never talk back to me again."

Triggers

I'm finding that my first exposure to an experience has me reeling inside. Subsequent exposures create less of a response. When I came for my interview, I saw an inmate in his unform. White with wide black stripes. I found it unsettling. It was indicative of dark history. Now I don't think twice about it. At another point I was holding a styrofoam box containing my lunch as I waited for the elevator. When the doors opened, it was packed with inmates and one officer. "You can get in if you want to." I hesitated for a second and then got in. As I stepped into the elevator, I intentionally left my fears behind.

Mental Health Unit

I work in the mental health unit. This is where the most violent and irrational inmates are housed. There are pods A – D. Those in A are the most mentally disturbed. Those in B are on suicide watch. These inmates are stripped naked and have a blue blanket if they choose to cover themselves. The blue gown is of heavy quilted material with Velcro to close it. This is known as the "turtle suit" by the inmates. When I saw my first naked inmate my eyes widened. Now it is commonplace to me. C pod is the largest and holds the relatively stable inmates. And lastly D pod holds inmates that are not capable of being around others. They are unstable or violent.

In B pod I worked with an inmate for days getting his medications and treatments to his satisfaction. I thought we were good. Then he yelled "Hey Nurse!" I turned and he was holding his limp dick in his hand. I was thinking "I'm not impressed." It was too early on in my job for me to say it out loud. I turned back to what I was doing. Now when I give medications to this pod, I am completely indifferent to if they are covered or not. Recently an inmate made a boa type scarf out of toilet paper and was prancing naked around his cell, the white paper in contrast to his dark skin. If they take their medications from me, I am happy. That is all that matters.

Another first didn't faze me. The A pod is pitiful and frustrating. These men can be cooperative for days on end and then scream about aliens causing their incarceration. I have a very poor sense of smell. As a nurse I couldn't be happier about it. We were moving from the B pod to the A pod, and I was astounded that I could smell such a stench. When the door was opened the smell was powerful and overwhelming. A brown liquid covered half of the upper tier. Two small plastic bags were among the wreckage. They had taken the plastic bags their sandwiches came in and filled them with feces. The officers ascending the stairs were vehemently yelling and cussing into their black jackets that covered their noses. Many years ago, I cared for a young man with a colostomy bag who was very talkative. I taught myself not only to shut off the scent but to be able to talk to him in my normal voice. I felt he needed that. From that experience, I was able to bound up the steps with nothing covering my nose. I gave medications to those I needed without difficulty. Inmates throw feces under their cell doors and smear their windows. Is it out of aggression, attention seeking, or psychotic reasons? Who can say.

Restraint Chair

I had witnessed inmates in a metal restraint chair with nylon straps when I was in training. They also are required to wear a spit mask, so I cannot see their entire face. But then it became my job to assess them on my own, making sure that the restraints are not too tight, checking their blood pressure, making sure they are okay and documenting their behavior. My first encounter was in the women's unit. The women cause me more anxiety than the men. There are inmates who look like they should be home baking cakes but instead have a relentless drug addiction. I approach the woman in the restraint chair. "I done pissed on myself four times!" I look at her jeans soaked with urine. I flash a look at the officer. She mumbles something apologetically. I later learned that if the inmate is in the restraint chair, they cannot use the restroom. I am astounded. I must check on this woman every fifteen minutes for the first hour. She yells, cusses, and hopes that me and all my grandchildren die. Nice. On my next visit she is sleeping. I don't see any top teeth. The bottom teeth are extremely small and black. At one point she becomes calm. "I see that you're quiet" I say, "Would you like to come out of the chair?" She quickly turns her head away. I saw the officer assigned to her in the cafeteria a few days later. She told me that the inmate said she had been drunk and high and she apologized profusely for her behavior.

Next, I had a male in B pod to assess in the restraint chair. There are restraints on the shoulder, arms, wrists, and ankles. Invariably the wrist restraints are too tight. I have been trained to be able to put two fingers under the wrist restraints. I have been taught that if they are tighter than that I have the authority to have them loosened. I call for them to be loosened and I am met with resistance, but it is done. I check in with the department head and she assures me that I am doing the right thing. When I return to the inmate his wrist restraints are sinched back down. I tell them to loosen them again. When I returned a third time the wrist restraints were tight again. "What the hell is going on here?" I say. They mention that they are calling their boss because they are frustrated with me.

I returned to my area working on gathering my medications. The Sargent did not show up. My boss came to me and was sweet as she could be. She told me that the two-finger rule for the tightness of restraints was unrealistic. Violent inmates could have the restraints tighter. Inmates purposely lift their elbow to make the restraints look tighter than they are. She told me that I have never seen an inmate escape a restraint chair or I would understand. I kept trying to tell her what the department head had said. She was dismissive and talked over me. She was siding with the officers while throwing me under the bus. It was done so sweetly. Later in the day she could tell I was still upset. She wanted me to come to her office before I left so we could talk it over. I didn't stop in.

When I got home, I went on Google and YouTube looking for inmates escaping restraint chairs. There were none. There were only stories of police brutality and inmate deaths. I wasn't scheduled to work for three days. When I returned, the corrections staff seemed exceptionally nice to me. One officer followed me into my area and asked me if I was doing okay. I asked why the concern. He just said that he was being kind. I had made sure that I wasn't going to talk about the officers that were involved. I hoped that all this would pass over and not be a problem. Now I know that as with all jobs, what I am taught and what takes place are two different things.

Administrative Segregation

Today I had to talk with the inmates that were in "Admin Seg", meaning that they were deemed by the administration to be segregated from the general inmate population because of their reckless behaviors. This was my first time doing this task. I decided that I would tell them that I am the nurse from mental health, and I am checking in to see if they had any medical or mental health issues. All sixteen inmates were pleasant and cooperative. At one point I had to return to my area. I told the mental health counselor that a man wanted to be seen because he was hearing voices. I got the response I anticipated. "He is seen twice a week. That is sufficient." She was concerned about her hair and what she would have for lunch. I returned to the cells with Tylenol and two pitiful books in answer to an inmate's request to read something that will help him be a better man. Several had a laundry list of issues. One suffered a head injury more than once and there were side effects that probably would not improve. One young man had multiple mental health labels. One of the last inmates I interviewed told me that he was restless and claustrophobic in his cell. He didn't know what to do about it. I said I would explore some options. Back at my desk I poked around in his files. He had two murder charges. He was yet to be 25 years old. Claustrophobia will be a lifelong struggle for him.

Suicide Watch

Inmates who are feeling suicidal are brought to the mental health unit to be assessed. They are either put on suicide watch in B pod or they are sent back to their floor. Mental health counselors are supposed to do this assessment, but if they are not available either myself or a medical nurse takes over. I was the only one left in the mental health unit when I took the call. An inmate on the 4th floor was suicidal. I went to the medical unit to get advice. I was told to call the officer and have the inmate sent to our unit. After a few minutes, a young man with a huge grin on his face appeared. I thought of my friend who attempted suicide and of all the celebrities who have succeeded. I listened to the charge nurse talk with him for a while. He was all smiles. I said, "I don't have time for this" and left. I learned that this is common. When he found out that he would be stripped down naked in a cell, he changed his mind and went back to the 4th floor. Inmates state that they are suicidal in order to leave their floor. Maybe they have borrowed money and can't pay it back. There are many scenarios, sometimes the least of them is suicide.

After Work Sights

As I left work this evening, I saw what appeared to be a prostitute. She was talking on her cell phone. She did not spend time by the curb. She had on short shorts presenting her shapely legs. She walked with ease in her high heeled shoes and gracefully moved in large arcs. The funny thing was that she was walking on the side and in front of the courthouse. It was a strange backdrop; I wonder who she was talking to.

Another day a lady in a bikini was dancing wildly in front of the courthouse. Many sketchy things happen in front of the courthouse. The jail is directly across the street. But there she was, doing her craze as I was heading to my car. I asked about her at work the next day. Oh yes, she was in jail. She had been high on meth.

June

Lunch Lady

I go to the ODR (Officers Dining Room) for free meals every day. One worker gives me a dark scowl every time she waits on me. I am patient because I am sure she is sick of people coming through here for a month, never to be seen again. What is the use of getting to know you? Get your food and get out. It got a little tedious at times. She would break into a radiant smile as she joked with the person in front of me. Her face would snap shut when I approached. One evening I was very busy. I rushed into the ODR and she gave me a huge grin. "It's 6:02. We're closed."

Lilly

I took the elevator from the second to the third floor to visit the female held in the restraint chair. This wasn't my first visit with her. She had been in the restraint chair on multiple occasions. She was a relatively attractive brunette. This time she had painted her face with her menstrual blood. "I'm an Indian!" she said with glee. She was always happy. She regularly made comments to me such as "I really like your titties." I had never been hit on by a woman before, it was unnerving. She told me at one point that she was going to behave. And she has. She's out of the lock down unit, into a unit that allows socialization, television and other things. Good for her.

Wound care

I have always enjoyed doing wound care. The jail puts a real twist on this skill. I care for inmates with gunshot and stab wounds. These inmates are usually not allowed out of their cells. I must anticipate which supplies to bring into their dark cells. My techniques have evolved over time. Now I have the pleasure of seeing questionable wounds heal nicely.

Chest pain

An inmate was complaining about chest pain. I arrived at the scene and could tell that he was in severe pain. He couldn't walk down the steps, he had to be carried. I assumed that the inmates would be concerned for him. No. Several of them yelled loudly "Nurse, nurse!" They didn't care at all; they just wanted my attention. He clearly needed to go to the hospital, but instead they loaded him up with Ativan. Cost savings rather than sending him out to the hospital.

The Perfect Turd

We have vertical poles all along the top tier of our units. They are to prevent inmates from jumping over the railing to try to harm themselves. They call them jumpers. The last one jumped feet first. He incurred serious injuries to his legs. Later he furiously insisted that the jail should pay for all his medical bills.

Inmates throw feces, urine and spit out of their pass thru doors where they receive food and medication. They hope to hit the officers mainly or anyone else who happens to walk into their line of fire. Sometimes they smear it all over the cell window. But this particular day was unique. As I mounted the stairs, I spotted the perfect turd. It was lodged dead center between the poles and there it stayed.

Street Clothes

New inmates should come to the unit in their jail uniform. If not, they have been unruly in the intake process. Many are brought to the jail while they are under the extreme influence of drugs and alcohol. They can't even understand the charges against them. When I peek in a cell and see jeans, I know it has been a rough landing. The funniest thing I have seen so far is an inmate smiling through the cell window with his sunglasses on. What a sight. Somehow, they let him keep them, and he wore them constantly. He wore them during an extensive meeting with his lawyer. I heard they were very expensive, thousands of dollars and that was why he got to keep them. I asked him one day how much he paid for them. Under ten dollars.

Roof Basketball

I was on the fifth floor visiting some inmates. As I neared the elevator to return to my floor, I saw sunlight coming from a doorway. I discovered steps that led outside. Soon a sergeant came in the stairwell. She took me outside on the rooftop and I saw several basketball hoops and bleachers for the spectators. Several lively matches were in progress. I was amazed. It was a beautiful summer day, and these guys were blowing off steam. She told me how most of the staff are against it. And this was the South building. I am in the North building; we don't have it at all. The staff in the North building completely blocked it. Why can't they see that letting them play basketball will make their job easier?

Officer Becomes Porter

Porters stay out of their cell all day. They are the most trusted of the lot. They work on the units distributing meals and cleaning cells. Workers have their length of stay reduced in exchange for their labor. A particular porter was sexually involved with youth and had several charges concerning child pornography. Then I found out that he was a former officer at the jail.

Is this some sick male comradery that shows empathy towards him?

July

The Numbers Give It Away

Inmates are given a number consisting of seven digits. The first three numbers really tell the story. All our current inmates' numbers start with 175. The last four digits do not mean much to me. If an inmate's number starts with 173 then they have been at the jail for years. This usually is the case for murder, with legal battles that become drawn out. Once settled they are transferred to prison; "riding out" as they say. I know several in their twenties in this boat.

Ridin' Out

We are a jail, which is supposed to be a place of temporary housing. Some inmates receive their final sentence and move on to prison, where they will serve a lengthy sentence. Others are released. We had a temperamental and violent inmate that was being moved to a prison up north, probably for murder. Somehow, I had a rapport with him. I told the officers who were gathered in our unit about that. They were thrilled and had me go in with them. He was difficult, but not what we were expecting. He did not give me any eye contact, pretended I wasn't there. Out he went. Soon after I had to visit a different floor. The elevator opened and there they were, they hadn't left yet. He saw me, and as plain as day he gently said, "Bye Miss Leila."

Religion

Plenty of Muslims here. This gentleman is tall, with long black hair. But his skin is very light, and he has bright blue eyes. It's one of many things I have learned here is that men can choose to become Muslims and change their entire name. They say he had a tattoo removed from his forehead that said "I love whores". Now he is very pleasant and cooperative. I just want to say, "Hi Steve!", his real name.

Plenty of Christians here. Lots of talk about Jesus and the whole Christian bag. Invariably they descend into bad behavior. Screaming, yelling, kicking their cell door for hours. The last time this happened the inmate screamed at the Corrections Officer "suck my dick." I was able to go to his cell and say, "Well that doesn't sound like a good Christian man." "You're right, I am so sorry. God bless you, god bless you." He apologized to the Officer. I'm sure that compliant attitude will stay in place for at least ten minutes.

Gettin' High

Inmates have been consumers of all kinds of drugs on the outside. They are used to having a buzz. They still get plenty of drugs on the inside, more prolific than on the outside I am told. But then they get in a pinch to get high. "Tuning" is the thing. Pieces of paper are sprayed down with bug spray. Then they roll the paper and smoke it. Three inmates were brought to our unit that had been tuning. One was in a restraint chair with low blood pressure. The second one was sent back to his floor. The third was in a cell. I went over to peek at him. "I need water." I reminded him that there was a water fountain in his cell. "But it's not acting right!" I told him to push the button to let me see what it was doing. "No!" he cried in a frightened voice. Who knows what he saw in that stream of water.

The Popcorn Machine

I saw a man pushing a cart that reminded me of a popcorn machine. I asked him about it. Inmates get legal mail, mainly from their lawyers. The letters are copied, and the original is shredded. Lawyers send drugs imbedded in their correspondence. The popcorn machine is to deflect the misdeeds of lawyers and other outsiders. Astonishing.

Set Free

Walking to my car after work I saw three paper bags on the sidewalk. Down to the left near an entrance to another street there were three flip flops. Three friends had been released from jail together. Happy trails, I hope you can build a good life for yourselves.

ABLE Training

Active Bystandership for Law Enforcement (ABLE) Project. I went to this training and was the only nurse there. All were law enforcement officers. We heard many scenarios where the police made a bad decision, and no one stepped in because of feeling intimidated by their superiors. They tried to foster an environment where peers and outsiders would speak up and intervene. Excellent concept. But there is a huge problem. The officers in the jail are on mandatory overtime, many working 16 hour shifts. They are sleep deprived therefore, they are angry and discouraged. Arguments come easily. How can they make competent decisions in that state? There is no end in sight. In all my years of employment, never have I seen such appalling treatment of employees.

The Sandwich

I had been trying to give medications twice a day to a particular inmate. He always refuses. He was yelling things that could not be understood. He reminded me of a crazed animal that could never be tamed. One thing that came out clearly was "You white, old bitch". Always a great start for my day. He was not allowed time out of his cell. I got the idea to give him a sandwich if he took his medications. It was a slow start, but it worked. After several weeks I asked one of the officers how he has been doing since taking his medications more often. "Well, he stopped yelling all day, sometimes he naps, and he doesn't piss on himself anymore." That was progress. When I came to his cell he would be at the door, readily taking his pills. He formed sensible sentences and talked with me.

One morning when I came to his cell, he was wrapped in a blanket, facing the wall. He refused his medications. Later I was looking through my emails and saw one from my coworker. No more sandwiches are to be given to him. You can't have a reward system. If you give something to one, all inmates will expect the same. There has to be a doctor's order for an inmate to get saltines (when taking antibiotics) so a sandwich is out of the question. I understand all the arguments. But to change a savage-type man into one that calmly communicates by way of a mystery meat sandwich seems like the right choice.

August

Family Crimes

He has white hair and beard. He makes a Santa-like thought cross your mind. He is supposed to have his blood pressure taken twice a day. Usually happens once. His blood pressure has a history of being very elevated. I give him 4 – 6 blood pressure pills every day. He also has three different inhalers. Really? There is only one or two psych meds in the mix, why don't you get transferred to another floor? I had heard of the stereotype that old white men come in here because of some sexual offense. He fit the bill. Rape of a girl under age 13. But then I saw on some electronic notes that it was his granddaughter. And that he is depressed because "I'm afraid my family will completely abandon me."

I deal with men in their twenties that have murdered more than once. Their home environment most likely created that mess. Another inmate has murdered several times and is bat shit crazy as they say. Maybe if he was on the correct meds at the time it wouldn't have happened. I can have patience with these. But a white man with lifelong depression being the most serious problem he has, and rapes his granddaughter? As I give him more medications than anyone on the unit, I feel disgusted. His cellmate was worried about him, that he had a stroke based on the looks of the right side of his face. I did not see anything amiss. *Giving you all these meds, inhalers, fuck you dude. I hope you stroke out.* But then I had a change of mind. Let's keep you going as long as possible. After some time spent at our jail you will ride out to prison. Hopefully it is several states away for your family's sake. When you arrive at the prison as the newcomer, all will know your crime. You will get special treatment from the inmates for the rest of your useless life.

A different inmate had raped his daughter. He was interviewed in our office. I didn't listen to it much. He had wealthy relatives that could bail him out. Oh, but wait a minute, you don't have a bond. Looks like you are stuck with us.

Teacher Pandering Child Porn

He came from a nice suburban school district. He appeared to be intelligent. He said that his girlfriend is supportive of him. (At this difficult time.) The oddest thing was that he was relaxed. Even when he went into the larger unit where the muscular, rather unstable tough guys were, he seemed comfortable.

In retrospect he was probably comfortable knowing that his expensive lawyer was going to get him out after only ten days.

October

Entitled

The new inmate was asking for bottled water or Gatorade, he couldn't drink the water here. And the cell walls are dirty, he complained, they must be washed before he would go in. Had he served time in Norway or Sweden?

Hospital Run

"I need to go to the hospital!" The reasons that inmates want to go to the hospital: lots of attention, good food, clean sheets, and the ability to make phone calls to their people.

Thicker Skin

I withheld a med because this inmate always told me to take it back. This evening, he wanted it and screamed "You bitch, suck my dick." Amazingly it didn't faze me. I went back to my desk and logged in the meds that I had given. When I got to his name, I got the med that he wanted and went out to find an officer. We woke him up, but he gladly came to the door to get the pill. He thanked the officer, not me. Through all of this I didn't get upset. There are many reasons for this, or I can blush and think that I grew an inch taller as a jail nurse.

Stephanie

One of the prettiest women I know, my boss, sat down gingerly on my desk. "I need your help. I need you to draw up an emergency injection for a female inmate." "I hate those, because it requires two injections" I said. "That's fine, we will tag team her and give her a shot in opposite arms. Afterwards, we need to give her a bath in the restraint chair." I jumped into action to get the injections ready. The female's name resonated in my head; I had checked on her when she was in the restraint chair during an earlier incarceration. I tried to bring up her face in my mind, to retrieve anything at all. No luck.

I went with my boss and two others upstairs with a cart loaded with the things we needed. Officers were lined up on both walls in their SWAT team gear of shields and helmets. (In our jail they are called the CERT team.) The leader spoke and told of their mission while the camera rolled. We were called in once she was secured in the restraint chair. Her head was covered with a spit mask, so I could not see her face. After her restraints and her vital signs were checked we moved in to give the injections. I spoke to her as I was giving her the injection, but she did not respond. After the injections were complete, the CERT team left. Now it was time to bathe her. She had been in jail for 14 days and had stopped eating and caring for herself. She had her street clothes underneath the jail uniform. I thought that the officer would loosen one strap at a time and let us remove her clothes. No, we had to use scissors. My boss and another woman began cutting her clothes. I busied myself with washing her exposed areas. If I let down my guard for a second, I could smell the deep stench that emanated from her. But many years ago, I taught myself the skill of not only cutting off the stench but talking and carrying on a conversation in a normal voice.

She had extensive amounts of urine and feces in her clothes. As I kneeled to wash a particular area the flashback came in full force. I felt as though the wind had been knocked out of me, because I remembered who she was. She was a frail and timid woman who trusted no one and would not speak. Last time she finally opened up to me and, in a half-whispered voice told me how she had been raped several times during the night. I had tried to explain to her that she was here with all females, but she wasn't having it. After today's encounter I learned

that she was homeless. Now it all made sense.

The others would cut the clothes, and I would position myself as best I could to pull off

the large pieces. The second cuttings were too drenched in urine and liquid feces that I did not

have the strength to pull them out. They did more cuttings. Finally, we were down to the

underwear and bra. The bra was nothing but a thin, short camisole so we decided to leave it.

We cut off her underwear. I saw a white silvery thing that turned out to be tampon string. Her

labia looked strange. The same silvery tampon string appeared to crisscross up the labia like a

ladder. Thoughts came in my mind of what abuse has been done to female genitals in other

countries. My boss took over and she asked the woman if she could clean her. The woman said

no. I wouldn't have asked, a tampon left in surrounded by filth was sure to cause an infection.

We covered her with sheets and let the officers remove her from the restraint chair. Then she

got dressed in her uniform and was put back into her cell. On my evening med pass, one of the

women that had been with us knew I would be glad to hear that Stephanie had taken out her

tampon on her own.

December

True Psych

There was a lot of commotion in the sallyport. I was asked to assess a man who had been fighting. He had his arms handcuffed behind his back. His lower lip was bleeding. I learned that he fought the officer who was trying to put him back into his cell after his "hour out". If they are reasonable, inmates can get an hour or more out of their cell each day on the mental health unit. Who knows how long it had been since this inmate was out. He was still quite angry, yelling insults. I was not able to determine the extent of his injuries because of his behavior. His blood pressure was high. At one point he stood up and they angrily slammed him back into the plastic chair. Some of what he was saying didn't make sense. They moved him to the restraint chair.

Once in the chair he mistook me for someone he knew. "My dear Helen," he said with relief. "Why are all these people in my house?" I told him that it was cold outside. He asked me several questions about his situation, and I gently answered. I took his blood pressure again and it was perfect.

I looked at his files. He was a homeless, schizophrenic man in his early thirties. He is out of touch with reality, and we are demanding that he responds in the way that we want. I could see that all the answers I gave to his questions would not take place. He trusted me. I couldn't wait to get off work and ditch the feeling that I had betrayed him. I insinuated that he would be treated well.

Another Visit

One of my tasks is to visit inmates that are in high security lockdowns because of their behavior. The main reasons are assaulting an officer and vandalizing their cells. Many have burnt holes in their windows to receive drugs from the outside, like Rapunzel letting down her hair.

Today was no different. Two inmates showcased their penises. I am not sure what they hope to gain. I find it annoying and counterproductive. I needed to follow up on the issues we had talked about last time.

An inmate was out of his cell using the phone. He said that he had no idea why they treated him so badly. He nodded at his wrists and ankles. They were handcuffed and shackled. He said he would never kill anything or let anything die. Why do they treat him that way? He and the officer were laughing. I checked his record when I got back to my desk. It was hard to tell if he was wanted for one or several murders.

Another inmate told me in low, deep tones that he couldn't wait to get out. He wanted to cut and stab with a knife. He kept saying it with various versions. He got to me; I was nervous. I was just getting ready to look at the officer across from me when the inmate exclaimed loudly "I want a steak!" There was laughter all around.

Intensive Management Unit (IMU)

This unit is the most restricted of all units in the jail. My job is to visit this unit weekly to see if they have any medical or mental health needs. They cannot have anything as far as word searches and such. Today an inmate was telling me that he was "barely holding on." They are in their cells 23 hours a day, no TV, nothing to occupy their time. He was seriously pleading his case, while others were joking around. He continued to state his plight, although in quite a good-natured way. An officer I had never met before chimed in. "Well, I could give you some tips on how to kill yourself." There was awkward laughter.

Waiting

I am completely dependent on the officers. I can't do anything without them as far as interacting with the inmates. I spend a lot of my time waiting. They all know what I want, usually a medication pass. Yesterday I waited while they finished their conversation about mythical horses.

January

A Matter of Race

I had another customer in the restraint chair today. He came up to our floor angrily yelling through his spit mask. He came straight up from intake, the entry point from the street to the jail. The street clothes we see are something else. He had no shirt on. His chest was riddled with tattoos. There were several large roses among the mix.

I must check on him every fifteen minutes for the first hour. During the first check he told me his story. He went into a chili parlor and asked to charge his phone. A staff member came out from the back in a wild tear. Problems ensued and he left. Once outside, three policemen with their hands on their hips were approaching him. He was afraid of being shot, so he ran. He was shot with a taser in his leg which was still hurting. He told me the story on my next check as well. "What would you have done?" he asked. "Well, if I wasn't guilty, I wouldn't have run." I said. "That's because you're WHITE!" he yelled. "You think because it's 2023 things are better. They're NOT!" I tried to let him know that I agreed with him. I was drowned out by the inmates in the surrounding cells yelling out at the same time variations of "fuck you bitch". "I think they want me to leave." I said. He seemed disappointed. Supposedly he started arguments with the officers nearby. There was a volley of insults between them. "All those officers in there are terrible, she's the only one that's cool." I heard him say.

Hopeless

He is a black man with long dreadlocks. He has a pleasant face with the eyes of an innocent boy. He is only 32 years old. Homeless. Schizophrenic. Slim contact with reality. No emergency contacts. No contacts at all. What is to become of him?

Customer Service

I was trying to check the blood pressure on an older black man. He was angry that we woke him up. The blood pressure machine didn't register. "I have to take it again with this" I said as I pulled the manual blood pressure cuff forward. All the sudden he yelled out "I'll beat your ass, bitch!" "Who are you talking to?" I asked calmly. "Somebody else." We continued.

The Mental Health Assessments

I overhear mental health professionals perform assessments in the office where I work. A young man stated "I've been shot three times, stabbed twice, jumped from a bridge and broke both femurs, had seven toes blown off and was electrocuted. I think that's why I have so much anxiety." Could very well be.

An older man stated, "My father was 8 years old when I was born." Kids these days.

Nightfall

As I walk to my car after my shift, the sound of my footsteps causes the mice and the rats to scurry for cover.

Confessions

I was caring for a female in the restraint chair. "I sucked Trump's dick and got him into the Whitehouse, and he still hasn't done anything for me." We understand.

February

Loving

"I *LOVE* people" the inmate said. "That's great." I replied, keeping to myself that I don't necessarily share his sentiment. "I'm a cannibal!" he quipped.

The Doc

Our mental health doctor has been seeing inmates and drug abusers for decades. He is rather eccentric. He does Civil War reenactments as a hobby. We had a run- in early on, but now we're fine. Yesterday an inmate came out of his office and looked straight at me "He said I am full of shit! What kind of doctor says that?" In my head I was thinking "Ours."

Advocate

One of the roles of a nurse is to advocate for the patient. Most of the time when I suggest something for the inmate's benefit, the response I get is "Fuck him." So helpful.

Cocaine

"Is cocaine even a thing anymore? Is it even made these days?" the inmate asked sincerely. What did his drug test reveal? Positive for cocaine.

Martin

I am embarrassed to say that I was upset that I didn't get to talk with this inmate before he "rode out" as they say. He served 3 years in jail and now he was to serve 22 years in prison. He was in maximum security, and I had visited him on and off for nearly a year because of my job duties. He was quiet, hard to get to know. It turned out he had a dark humor about him and would joke about things that were serious. He was forced to come to the suicide watch section of the mental health unit because the new counselor took his jokes seriously. He was upset and asked for my help. The mental health director told me I was being manipulated. I had known him for a long time, they didn't know him at all. He got out of our unit about a day and a half later. A few days after that he rode out. He told someone that he was sick of the jail and was looking forward to prison where there are a few more perks. Good to see someone accepting rather than resisting their fate.

Requests

"Can you see if the officers can warm the water that comes into our cell a little bit? I'm cold when I am taking my bird bath!" he said while waving his hands all about.

March

As of the 29th I have been working at my new job for a year. It has been such a good experience that I do not plan on working anywhere else. At the same time there are a lot of things that are troubling. I reiterate the statement from my interview "When you walk to your car at night, your back won't hurt, your feet won't hurt, it's all a mental thing." Recently I found the comment below.

Is jail for rehabilitation or for punishment?

*Some correctional systems use punishment as the primary approach, others stress rehabilitation, and some use both punishment and rehabilitation, but **no current system focuses on incarceration as a short period of punishment followed by a lengthy period of community-based rehabilitation and strict supervision.***

I have seen an inmate in maximum security released straight to the street. Our website claims that we have GED classes and programs that help them at the time of release. I haven't seen any of these things being a strong force. I am making yet another attempt to get books to the inmates.

The age-old attitude toward mental health still exists. If an inmate has mental health issues, they will wait generally 30 days to get any professional help. Oh, but if it's a cardiac medication for high blood pressure they will get it on day one. On the psych unit, many of our inmates do not have any medications at all.

I used to be happy when one of the sickest inmates in our psych unit was transferred to an outside behavioral facility for a temporary stay. I thought that the worst ones were chosen to get intense psychiatric treatment for their good. But after a year I learned the truth. They are sent out in order to get them to the place where they appear sane enough to stand trial. Their quality of life after the trial is not a concern.

I am learning that I am a teeny cog in the giant wheel of justice. I give my suggestions. I am met with a smiling face while they are writing down what I said. "I will get back to you on this." I don't hear a thing, not even a rejection. I'm learning not to ask, to keep those thoughts to myself.

I am just one person. My attitude is helpful to some. I do little things that the inmates ask for, a word search, crackers with a medication, doing my best to get their requests to see a doctor pushed up on the list, smiling, joking, treating them as humans.

It's not all spreading rainbows and sunshine. I am called a bitch and worse on a daily basis. And there are the ones who turn on me after months of positive interaction. I have learned to have thicker skin. But most of all, personal growth can happen. Not one day is the same as the one before. New situations and various combinations happen daily. I must remain fluid and levelheaded. If I'm angry I have lost control of myself. I'm a different person from a year ago. In my personal life I have more confidence with difficult people. I have a richer life because of my experiences as a Jail Nurse.